Train
Time

by Katrina Streza

Hardcover ISBN: 978-1-5324-3749-6
Paperback ISBN: 978-1-62395-003-3
eISBN: 9781623952884
Images licensed from Fotolia.com
First Edition
Published in the United States by Xist
Publishing
www.xistpublishing.com

xist Publishing

Trains have changed over the years.

But they still have whistles,

wheels,

and gears.

The very first train was run on water.

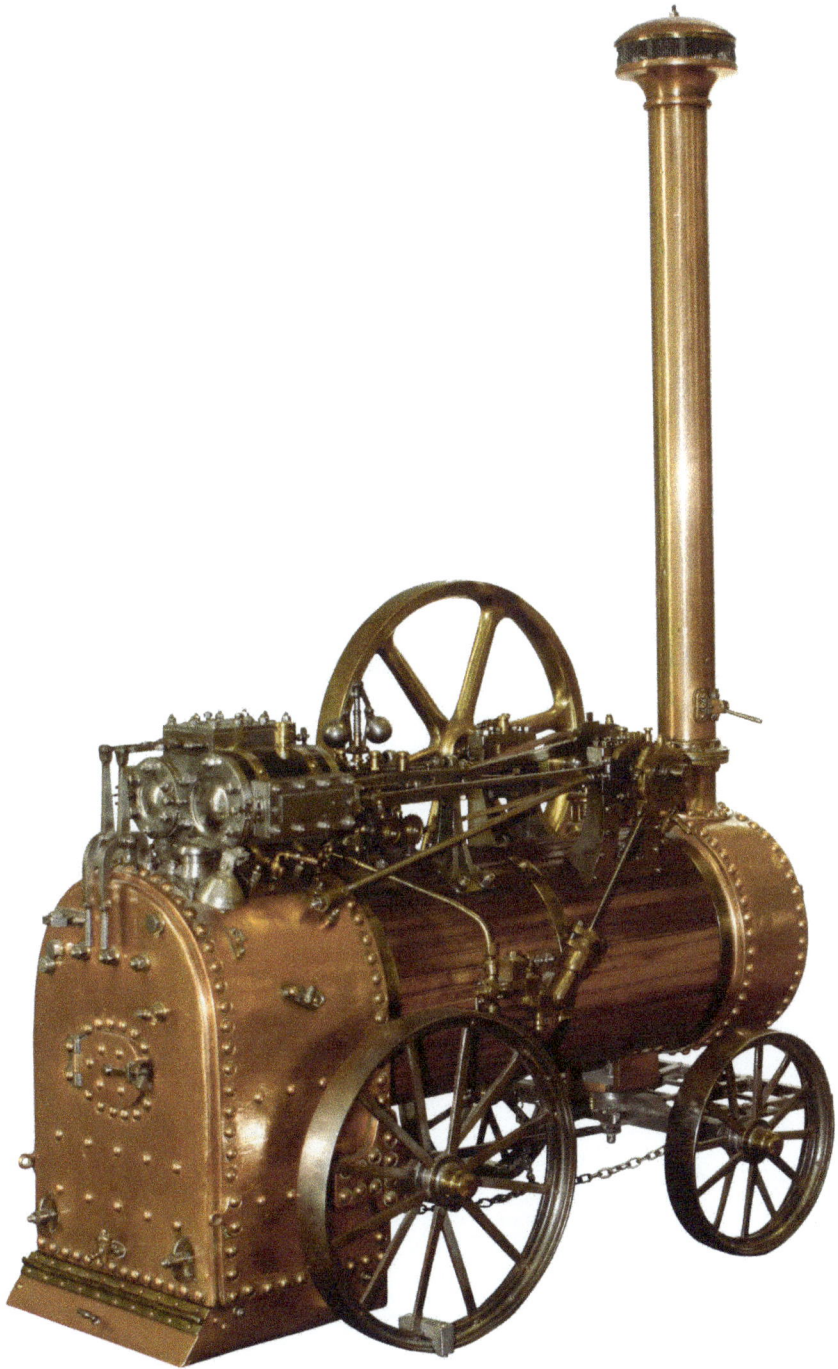

Then they used coal,

which got even
hotter.

Now, we use diesel
and gas to go fast

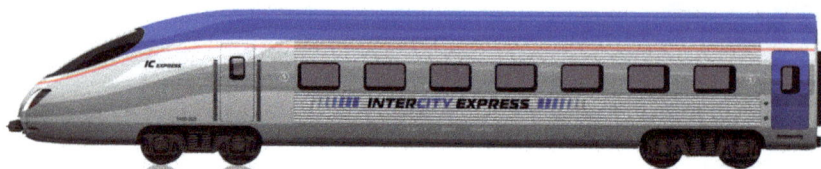

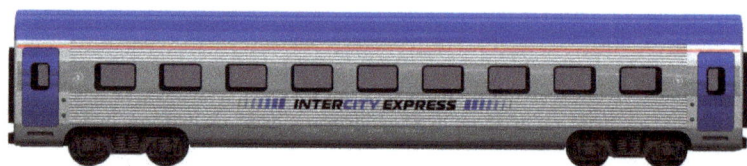

like high-speed
trains that often
zoom past.

Conductors use signs
to let people know

RAILROAD
CROSSING

STOP
ON RED
SIGNAL

when they should stop

and when they should go.

Kids play with toys

... and build their own trains.

182 001-8

People ride on tracks

instead of on planes.

Trains carry baggage,

people,
and food.

A ride on a train can brighten your mood!

www.ingramcontent.com/pod-product-compliance
Lightning Source LLC
Chambersburg PA
CBHW040417110426
42813CB00013B/2685